LIFE-GIVING LITURGIES

Arney's,
Thank you so much for
supporting me on this journey
and for helping make this
book a reality!
Love you guys!

— Haylen Haley
(Hobbs)

LIFE-GIVING LITURGIES

A GUIDE TO LEADING SMALL
GATHERINGS IN CREATIVE WORSHIP

Including pre-designed worship outlines and online resources

HAYDEN HOBBY

Life-Giving Liturgies
Copyright © 2023 by Hayden Hobby

First Edition

ISBN: 978-1-312-21033-2

TABLE OF CONTENTS

LITURGIES

Preface

When you grow up in the Bible Belt of America, going to church on Sunday mornings is as much of a given as showering or eating breakfast. It must be done regularly, and sometimes you enjoy it, but more often than not, you do it because going to church is what "good people" in the South do. Dogs bark, roosters crow, and Southerners sing "I'll Fly Away." In my family, however, church was more than a box to be checked ...

Faith always held a very meaningful and important place in our lives. Looking back on my childhood, it's clear that my parents wanted us to know and love God. Unfortunately, they struggled to find a church properly doing that itself. Deep down, I believe that they knew when a church was "off" or unhealthy, and as a result, we bounced around to a number of different churches over the years. None of these churches, however, were remotely liturgical or "High-Church" (an Anglican term for the priority of traditional sacraments and rituals). Because of this, I was familiar with only one type of worship service. The structure of that service was: sing some songs, the pastor preaches, then sing a couple more songs. In my adolescent mind, that was church. I knew that other styles of worship existed, but to me, they were stuffy, lifeless, and irrelevant. It wasn't until my second attempt at college at the age of twenty-two that I discovered the profound depth and beauty of these liturgical styles of worship. During this season of my life when I was coming to terms with the often unhealthy faith I grew up with, these traditional rituals of worship connected me with God and the Universal Church in an incredibly comforting and meaningful way.

During my second go at college as an undergraduate in Christian Formation and Worship, I became more intimately acquainted with the styles and formats of different church traditions. I learned how a well-written call to worship and prayer of confession can be powerful and I began writing some of my own, sharing them with the student body when I led worship for our chapel. I would regularly receive encouraging feedback from other students about how much they liked and connected with the prayers and calls to worship I wrote, and I could often observe this in action as a led worship. Watching my friends and peers engaged, and even moved, by what I wrote felt both humbling and empowering and is an experience I remember to this day. This college experience - learning to design and structure a good worship service, write powerful and convicting liturgy, and bring all of those elements together into a deeply formational worship service - completely altered the direction of my life.

My second college experience was marked by a lot of painful yet restorative spiritual healing, unlearning, and growth. While my parents had the best of intentions, many of the churches we attended were deeply broken, and over time, their brokenness broke me. I grew up in a hyper-conservative, simi-fundamentalist Christian community rife with misogyny, homophobia, toxic masculinity, and loads of shame. For three or four of my teenage years, we attended a church whose pastor my parents would later describe as a psychopath. While that specific church was the height of toxicity, my escape from this toxic Christian culture was neither quick nor easy. Coming into my time at John Brown University, I felt like the survivor of a sunken ship washed up on shore, battered and barely breathing.

My faith in a good, kind, and loving God somehow stayed intact, but my understanding of and hope in a healthy church community sank, crushed beneath an ocean of hypocrisy, bigotry, and hate. That ship needed a lot of work to ever sail again, so in the months and years following its destruction, I began slowly weaving together the old remaining planks of the sunken ship with new ones defined by God's character and with the shared labor of unlikely companions on my journey. During this time, writing songs, prayers, and liturgies helped me come to terms with my new perspectives on faith and also helped me share those perspectives with other shipwrecked castaways like me.

After putting in the work to construct my new, seaworthy ship of faith, I want to welcome others aboard and help them build their own strong and sturdy vessels out of good theology and practices about God, the Church, and ourselves. Therefore, it's my hope that the instruction and liturgies in this book help you, as a worship leader, facilitate healthy spaces of engaging, authentic, and Christ-centered worship where people can connect with God in a healing, transformative, and life-giving way.

The Whys of Worship

As a Southern-raised boy with little-to-no body fat, I abhor temperatures below fifty degrees. In the summer as a youngster, I would never last long in big, unheated swimming pools before my lips turned blue and my teeth began to chatter. Even today, as a grown man, if I know I'm going to be out in the cold for a long stretch of time, I will don an egregious number of layers trying to stay warm. If I'm going to brave the elements, it must be for something important. Worship, as I discovered during the pandemic years of 2020-2022, is one of those things.

My wife and I belong to a community called a house church (multigenerational small group) and, like the rest of the world, we had to figure out what it meant to be a community with literal masks on and required social distancing. No matter how necessary the precautions were, it was still challenging. When restrictions began to lift and people felt safer, summertime community activities weren't that difficult. We had cookouts, park days, and worship nights under the stars. Socializing outside and keeping our distance honestly felt pretty normal—like a breath of fresh air after so many months of isolation and anxiety. Then around mid-November it got cold, and as you now know, I hate the cold.

So, it was then November, it was cold, and guess what? We kept gathering outside together. I kept leading worship nights about once a month, which is crazy. Who wants to lead an awkward worship night with a bunch of people you haven't known for very long on a cold, wet, and windy November night? For any other activity, I would have said, "No, thank you. I'll kindly pass on that experience." But in this case, that wasn't an option. Worship is too important, and the opportunity to bring people into something I'm passionate about is something I just couldn't pass up no matter how cold it got. Even when I couldn't feel my fingers by the end of the night, in every shiver, in every chord sheet that blew away, and in every uncomfortable small-group-worship silence, it was worth it. While a little awkward at times, worship outside (even in the winter) offered those who participated the opportunity to experience God in a transformational way.

I have now led worship in a variety of spaces for almost a decade, and I often ask myself: why do we keep singing these songs week after week? For months and years, we play the same chords, memorize lyrics, and sway to the same melodies. Why haven't we followed in the footsteps of the Quakers, doing away with structured worship altogether? It would be a lot cheaper and take considerably fewer hours of planning and prep, but something about the rhythmic ritual of praising God continues to draw us in. There's something special about these poetic, Bible-breathed words that invoke honor and reverence for our living God - a beautiful power in our lungs as we declare our adoration in the presence of fellow believers.

Sometimes I worry we are just hooked on a feeling, addicted to the high of manufactured emotions that hold little in common with the work of the Holy Spirit. I often ask myself if we are simply passive participants on a cruise ship bound to break apart in the shallow waters of weak theology. At times, maybe. As worship leaders, the line between emotional shepherding and manipulation can be faint, often imperceivable to the untrained eye, and the danger is all too real.

On one side of the line, you're leading and directing emotions—not to control, but to guide people into a space where they can more readily encounter the Spirit of God. On the other side, you're sweeping people away into an induced state of hyper-emotionality driven by music, words, and lights (none of which are inherently bad). The excitement of that moment can feel so spiritual, but at the end of the day, it's frequently not. Emotion is an important aspect of worship, but the raw and unbridled emotional high produced by good music has little to do with God.

Any worship leader can fall for this tantalizing trap; I know for a fact that I've fallen for it many times in my career, especially in my earlier years of leading. The power to direct strong emotions in a large group is pridefully enticing. Participating in those big-group, collective emotions can be breathtaking, but I don't think the emotional high is why we *keep* singing. If feelings were the only driving factor of meaningful worship, then hymns would have long since passed away.

It's uncommon, in my experience, for a person's emotions to be deeply touched on their first time singing a hymn like "A Mighty Fortress Is Our God." However, far be it from me to say that this hymn has never connected with someone on a deep emotional level. In fact, I know that it has! But the deep-hearted response stirred by this song is not prompted solely by the music or the performance or the lights but because of the message and poetic comfort this classic hymn conveys.

That's why we keep coming back to songs like these. They put the words of faith, hope, and love into our mouths when we don't know what to say. When we don't know how to hold on to hope in a hopeless situation, these songs remind us how and why. When we don't know how to lament the brokenness of our world, these songs walk us through it. When we're hurt by the people in our lives that we thought would never hurt us, these songs verbalize how to forgive and love again. This is why worship is so important, and I believe that whether you're humming alone in your car, leading a small group, or singing in an auditorium with thousands, worship lies at the crux of our formation into the likeness of Christ.

As worship leaders, we are therefore tasked with a huge responsibility. We are the sages, the sherpas, the mountain guides and trailblazers, the ones directing the rope to which people cling as we guide them, walking altogether, up steep mountains and into the presence of God.

It might be easy to think that as the production and sets become larger and more extravagant, leading worship becomes more difficult. That has actually not been my experience. When the stage, the lights, and the crowd with whom you're engaging get bigger, it becomes easy to see yourself as a rockstar rather than a shepherd, and as everything intensifies, you quickly lose the intimacy that comes with singing eye-to-eye before ten or fifteen people. You're no longer a fellow participant but a distraction. Leading worship for a smaller group can be scary—people can *see* you—but so much depth of meaning and connection both with God and your community can be found in small-group worship.

If you're a musically talented person with no formal education in ministry or theology, leading worship in any setting can be a daunting task. It's a vulnerable position with a lot of attention, criticism, and opportunity for things to go wrong. Still, with a little guidance, anyone can lead a great worship service for a small group or house church. Direction and structure are perhaps the necessities some worship leaders do not have, and that's where I come in.

As with learning any craft, it takes time and consistent practice to become a good worship leader, and making some mistakes is part of the job. In spite of whatever bumps you hit on the way, this journey will equip you with the tools and motivation to step into this pastoral role, positively shaping your life and the lives of others into the image of Christ.

CHAPTER ONE

Full, Whole, Honest, and Creative

I've realized along my ever-winding path of faith that I primarily connect with God through my intellect and understanding. I love using my mind to think about and come to grips with the nature of God, the Trinity, salvation, atonement, and other biblical and theological themes related to faith. Studying God and His Word quickly became a beloved hobby and passion, which fueled my decision to attend seminary after completing my undergraduate degree. A seminary professor of mine pointed out that on some level, we're all theologians, meaning we all wrestle with the challenging questions of our faith and the lived reality of knowing and trusting God. This is part of what it means to follow Christ—to work out our faith even within our fear and doubt. This process is incredibly serious to me because I have experienced the harm that can come from bad theology. For that reason, every liturgy I write is intended to be theologically full, relationally whole, scripturally honest, and passionately creative.

Theologically Full

In something as subjective as learning about God and the Bible, the concept of good and bad theology may seem unhelpful. However, our understanding of something theological can be deeply personal, and the way we come to this understanding needs to be rooted in good methodology.

Good theology always points us towards the two greatest commandments declared by Jesus in Matthew 22:37-39, *"Love the Lord your God with all your heart and with all your soul and with all your mind.' This is the first and greatest commandment. And the second is like it: 'Love your neighbor as yourself'"* (NIV). If our theology is not actively helping us love God and informing the love of people in our lives, then it's bad theology. That means there's a lot of bad theology out there, and while the theology I present in this book is not going to be perfect, it is, to the best of my ability, written with love for God and others at its center.

Every worship experience I craft is dedicated to a theological theme or idea that challenges and transforms those who engage with it, nudging them toward a more full and embodied reflection of Christ. Through a combination of songs, prayers, confession, and Scripture readings, I hope everyone involved encounters important theological concepts like reconciliation, hospitality, and lament in ways that engage their heads, their hearts, and their hands. In other words, I want to create thoughtful worship experiences that invite people to bring every aspect of themselves to the table.

Relationally Whole

Relational wholeness speaks into how we live our day-to-day lives as God's image-bearers in the world, our cities, our neighborhoods, our churches, and our homes. In Matthew 22, Jesus speaks of how important loving the people in our lives is, second only to loving God. We are asked to literally "flesh out" and embody what it means to love people in the way that he loved. We are all in a constant process of learning how to show empathy and compassion, how to walk in someone else's shoes, how to cry with those who are mourning, and how to celebrate with those who are joyful. In the Gospels, Jesus teaches us that we ought to do all of these things, but it's our job *as leaders* to teach people how to follow those instructions in our present, modern-day context.

Every call to worship, every prayer of confession, and every original song points to the type of community I believe Jesus calls all of his followers to—one where all are unconditionally welcome, and where the love, grace, and forgiveness of God are named and experienced. The liturgies later in this book not only welcome and include that, but they also challenge many of the negative and un-Christlike behaviors we all so naturally tend to exhibit, whether that's pride, apathy, or prejudice. The idea is radical acceptance and inclusion as well as a challenge to love and live in an even more unabashedly Christlike way.

Scripturally Honest

When I say that I want my liturgies to be scripturally honest, I mean two things: first, I want every theme and theological concept to be inspired by and rooted in the truth of Scripture, and second, I want us all to be honest with ourselves about the lens we use to read and interpret Scripture. Humans are never unbiased; it's our nature. Being scripturally honest with ourselves means realizing that we all bring our own background, baggage, and beliefs into how we read and interpret Scripture, and that's neither good nor bad—it just is.

With this truth about ourselves in mind, humility is paramount. I grew up in a culture that believed their interpretation of Scripture was the one and only way to understand the Word of God, and not agreeing was akin to heresy. To disagree with the interpretation was to disagree with Scripture itself. However, this kind of thinking is detrimental to truly understanding the truth that our scriptures hold. We have to come to terms with the fact that other Christians see certain things differently, and not only are they equally loved by God but they may even teach us something new.

As you read my thoughts and liturgies, I ask you to put down your ego and any desire to be "right." God reveals new parts of who we are and who he is when we let go of our pride. If you find yourself agreeing with nothing or with everything in this book, I ask that you "check in" with yourself. Are you reading and worshipping with fresh, unexpectant eyes? Are you reading with uncompromising biases? Ask yourself, "What fresh, new word is God trying to speak to me today, and what might I hear if I truly give myself the space to listen?"

Passionately Creative

Creativity opens up otherwise unafforded pathways for divine encounters with our God, who can paradoxically be richly known through experiences in creation and Christ while at the same time being more mysterious and multifaceted than we could ever imagine. When it comes to truly understanding God, we're much like the cave-dwelling inhabitants of Plato's famous allegory in *The Cave*. Try as we might, we're simply incapable of experiencing anything but a shadow of who God really is. Not because God is purposefully withholding God's full self or, as in Plato's allegory, because we refuse to turn and face reality, but because we're limited beings who were created by a self-revealing yet incomprehensible God.

The fullness of God is beyond our limited human understanding, but we sometimes miss opportunities to probe deeper into the mystery of God by losing sight of our God-given creativity, curiosity, and imagination. Not everyone was born to be a painter, musician, or architect, but we're all creative in our own unique way. When we're able to get in touch with that creativity while worshiping our creative, creator God, we make space for the Holy Spirit to speak the truth of God's love, majesty, and justice to our hearts and minds in new and special ways. A few of my most beloved and powerful moments worshiping God were facilitated by a worship leader who boldly chose to be creative in their leadership, guiding those they led into a space where their assumptions were challenged and their imaginations were engaged.

It's my hope that the songs, prayers, and liturgies you find in this book will challenge your assumptions and engage your imagination, illuminating different angles and perspectives on God, and shining light in different and sometimes uncomfortable places. Occasionally, when our source of light becomes static and fixed, we get used to the one "shadow" that God cast, forgetting how many other shapes God may take if we let our imagination change the direction and location of the light. It's true that there are good and bad ways of thinking about God, but creativity says, "Let's leave the world of black and white for a moment and add a little color." Creativity makes no statements, it does not speak in absolutes, but simply invites the observer to wonder. Creativity asks many questions and gives very few answers, and that (along with many other things) is what I attempt to do in these liturgies. Take this as my invitation into an excitingly different and colorful world where God is even more loving, more forgiving, more mysterious, and more wonderful than before.

CHAPTER TWO

Work of the People for the People

I've always been fascinated by language, and as your average unilingual American, I often wonder what it would be like to fluently think and communicate in a language other than English. Language affects how we perceive and understand reality, for instance, some languages have words with no direct translation or meaning in other languages. These words often describe shared or universal human feelings or experiences, but are, at the same time, indescribable outside of their mother tongue. In Portuguese, the word "*saudade*" describes a sort of melancholic emptiness or longing—a feeling that something wonderful is gone and will never be known or felt again. However, there are no words in the English language that perfectly expresses what *saudade* means. The best we can do is use other words with similar meanings to try and sum it up.

Language also evolves, and the meaning of words will often change over time. The word "artificial," for example, was used in a bygone era to describe something full of artistic and technical skill. Today, the word "artificial" refers to something made by humans and often implies that it *reflects* something from the natural world. Words and language are not static nor always objective; they are simply tools of communication, and as such, the wielders have the privilege of deciding how those tools will be used. A tool may work on some tasks better than others, but (particularly in English), words are multitasking tools that work well in several contexts.

Words also often have feelings and memories attached to them, and the word "liturgy" or "liturgical" may, depending on your church background, conjure up feelings of comfort and familiarity or they may induce feelings of rigidity and pretension. Regardless of the feelings these words bring up in you, for the purposes of this book, I want to redefine them with a slightly different meaning. That is, I want to give the tool a slightly different task.

The original Greek word for liturgy, *leitourgia* (λειτουργία), is a composite word whose first part is derived from the Greek word for "people" (*laos*), and whose second part is derived from the Greek word for "work" (*ergon*). Together this word can be translated as either "work *of* the people," or "work *for* the people." Many intelligent people have argued this translation both ways, and each argument has a different implication on how we understand and execute Christian worship. However, I believe that the ambiguity of this word's translation is an invitation to acknowledge the truth behind each statement. The words that we write and say or sing together in a worship service are a work *of* the people, imagined and created by those who God entrusted with the talent and skills to create them—and are also a work *for* the people, inspired by God and presented by those who God entrusted with leadership over the body of Christ. This is one of the beautiful aspects of public worship! We, as the people of God, have the opportunity to humbly meet with and worship our God who leads us in worship while also allowing us to lead worship and be led by each other.

When it comes down to the nuts and bolts of what makes something a "liturgy" or "liturgical," every denomination that utilizes liturgical elements of worship will function in a slightly different manner, and many modern evangelical churches in America don't even want to touch the word "liturgy" with a ten-foot pole. That being said, I want to reiterate what I mentioned earlier in this chapter, which is that, for the purpose of this book, we're going to give the word "Liturgy" our own specific definition. For us, this word will mean, "the ordering and arranging of different elements of worship, which should include but are not limited to: songs, prayers, readings, a sermon or homily, communion, and baptism inspired by Scripture and the Spirit."[1]

While we most often associate the term "liturgy" or "liturgical" with Catholic or mainline protestant churches, every church has a Liturgy—a rhythm and order which dictates when and what happens in their worship service and in what typical order. Think about your church (or a church you have visited), for example. In what order do certain aspects of the service almost always take place? To quote the idea of my friend and fellow worship and culture theologian, David Bailey, "Every church has at

---

1   Note that if I use a capital L in "Liturgy," I'm referring to the structured service and arrangement as a whole, not the specific elements.

least an informal Liturgy, and that Liturgy reveals what a church values."

A worship service with a forty-five-minute sermon and only a couple of songs illustrates a church that places high value on teaching, but perhaps views sung worship as a lower priority. A worship service with a long passing of the peace or greeting time and a lot of space for mingling after the service illustrates a church body that places a higher priority on community interaction and hospitality than other aspects of a worship service. Remember, *Liturgy reveals what a church values.*

The Liturgy of any one church will always be slightly different from others because every church has different needs, and every leader has a different idea of what makes for a good worship service. If you visit two Baptist churches right across the street from each other, you may find that they share many elements in common, but they won't be exactly the same. That being said, there is a fundamental service structure that many well-rounded churches follow regardless of denomination or use of liturgical elements. This structure and the ideas that inform it are summed up well in the book *The Worship Architect* by Constance M. Cherry, but I believe they are ultimately inspired by the way that God consistently interacts with humankind in Scripture.

This pattern of worship outlined by Cherry involves a series of movements (I added the second movement) describing God's interactions with us and, in response, our interactions with God. The names given to these different movements are "The Gathering," "The Response," "The Word," "The Table," and "The Sending." A great example of this model in Scripture comes directly from the way that Jesus structured his ministry with his disciples while here on earth.

1. Jesus began by calling the disciples and gathering them to himself.
2. The disciples responded by dropping everything they were doing to follow Jesus.
3. After the disciples responded with this conscious decision to follow Jesus, he spent time teaching them about what it means to truly love and obey God.
4. Jesus spent most of his ministry teaching his disciples. Just before his death, he gathered them all at the table, where he shifted the Jewish Passover narrative literally and symbolically by offering his body and his blood, asking them to remember him by these elements in the days to come.
5. Jesus was then arrested, killed, and raised from the dead. With his last command to the disciples, he sends them out to make disciples of all nations.

In this formula set by the life and ministry of Jesus, we see a flow of relational exchanges between ourselves and God—a sequence of movements all initiated by God inviting us to respond. In the Gathering, God *initiates,* moving toward us by calling us to follow and worship. In the Response, we then move toward God by choosing to trust and obey. In the Word, God again moves closer toward us to teach us through the words preserved in Scripture, which give stories, poems, parables, and letters about what it means to love God and our neighbors. At the Table, again, we move toward God in response to hearing the Word by gathering to remember Jesus' sacrifice and subsequent victory over sin and death. Lastly, in the Sending, God commissions us through the words of Scripture and songs to go out into the world to be a light in the darkness.

"THE GATHERING" THEOLOGY

The Gathering marks the beginning of the communal conversation between God and God's people, and we start by acknowledging that it's God who invites us to worship. As human beings created in the image of God, we act with choice and agency, but when we show up to a worship gathering we are actively choosing to respond to a call that God has placed on our hearts - a call to gather with others in our community of faith and proclaim the goodness and provision of God in our lives. It's important that we take a moment at the beginning of a worship service to focus on why it is we've all come together in the first place. The first element you will see in most of the worship outlines in this book is what's known as a "call to worship," and this element of liturgy works as a kind of road map or launching pad, reminding us that we're here to respond to God's love and grace with worship.

"THE GATHERING" APPLICATION

You should start by welcoming everyone gathered together in a brief, warm, and inviting way—whatever feels most natural to the congregation. After this short acknowledgment of everyone's presence and value, take a minute or two to tell everyone what the time will look like that day. Here, at the beginning of the service, it's important to set the tone and succinctly elaborate on what this time together entails. Explain that you'll be singing some songs, praying, sharing, and meditating on Scripture. If people know what to expect, they're more likely to feel at ease. Don't dive into too much detail; simply try to convey peace, acceptance, and safety, letting people know that this is a hospitable, judgment-free space to be themselves. This is also a good time to let everyone know what is expected of them. Tell them if they will need to sit, stand, or kneel, or even where the bathroom is, and that it's okay to get up (or sit down) if they need to.

"THE RESPONSE" THEOLOGY

Following this call from God is our response. As we are confronted with the glory and love of the one who calls us to gather, we respond in praise and worship, and this adoration is generally expressed in the form of music and singing. Depending on your church's denominational leaning, worship might be expressed through exuberant dancing and shouting and, conversely, if you belong to one of the less charismatic denominations - whom I fondly refer to as "the frozen chosen" - you're usually pretty ecstatic to get a hand or two raised. Contrary to what some might say, however, outward expression is not, in and of itself, always a sign of genuine worship and connection with God. I believe that embodied worship is extremely healthy and important, but God always meets us where we are, so try not to be discouraged if those you're leading are not expressing their worship in the way that you might want or expect them to. Trust that God is working in the hearts of those you're leading in a way that's meaningful to them.

The second and equally important response to the revelation of the glory and love of God is humble confession and repentance of sin. We take a moment at this stage in our worship to publicly acknowledge our sins and shortcomings as a community before God and ask for forgiveness. This corporate confession is not only important in preparing our hearts for the rest of the worship service, but it is also a vital practice for the worshipping community as a whole. This is an opportunity to publicly confess our sins, and not just our private sins at that, but also the sins of our community, our nation, and our world. A church, small group, or house church that excludes the regular practice of confession and repentance will not be well equipped to accept and turn from the ways that it inevitably hurts and harms others and itself.

"THE RESPONSE" APPLICATION

In the pre-written Liturgies found in this book, the liturgical element of confession, like the call to worship, is broken up into sections read by the leader followed by sections read by everyone. These group prayers of confession might be the most unfamiliar and difficult element for the average worshipper. While private or individual confession is a well-known and practiced part of Western Christianity, communal or corporate confession is often under-taught, under-practiced, and poorly understood, especially in evangelical churches. Western culture is much more individualistic than other areas of the world, and as a result, American Christianity has often stressed the importance of confessing individual actions while struggling to connect with and confess the Church's complicity in brokenness that extends beyond the individual. It can be really hard to realize how we are implicated in the brokenness of what lies beyond ourselves. For this reason, it may require a little pastoral direction to lead people into a posture of truly engaging with a congregational prayer of confession rather than rejecting it as presumptuous or inapplicable. Here are some examples of words you could use to graciously introduce this type of confession:

"As we enter this time of corporate confession, remember that the purpose is not to guilt-trip or point out flaws, but to simply remind us of our collective brokenness and need for healing."

Or,

"This segment of responsive corporate confession is a great opportunity for us to practice confessing our sins to God and each other. While you may not personally struggle with or feel connected to every element of this confession, try to simply embrace the fact that we are all broken people in need of confession and repentance."

Biblical confession is intended for healing and is not a tool for condemnation; however, we all know that confession can be used or perceived in this way. For this reason, be careful and intentional about how you teach and use this powerful practice.

"THE WORD" THEOLOGY

It's important in every worship service—whether it's a huge church event or a small group gathering—that the Word of God is present. As we see in the Gospels, Jesus (the Word incarnate) spent a lot of time teaching his disciples and others, and while it can sometimes be tempting to just skip over Scripture when planning small-group worship events, we see through the life of Jesus that hearing the Word is a monumentally important aspect of being formed into the image of Christ. I personally have a complicated relationship with Scripture. I've seen it misused, weaponized, and compromised so many times and in so many ways that it feels difficult to know how to lead people in engaging with such a rich and complex text. But the beautiful thing is that in settings like these, you don't always have to give your opinion about a passage of Scripture or tell people how to apply it to their lives. You don't have to be a preacher. Sometimes all you need to do is present the Word and trust that God will work through it with or without your help.

"THE WORD" APPLICATION

This segment of the worship service can play out in different ways depending on you and your group's familiarity with Scripture. You might simply want to read through a passage of Scripture a few different times with different voices or translations; pose a couple of questions to think about while listening to the text; preface the passage; or you might want to jump right into it. Whichever path you choose, remember that you are not there to give a sermon but to help people engage with the Living Word of God to the best of your ability.

One practice of engaging with Scripture in small groups that I've found very helpful is *Lectio Divina*, which is the practice of quietly experiencing Bible passages - giving the words the opportunity to speak to the listeners themselves. In *Lectio Divina*, one person reads a passage of Scripture all the way through three different times. The first time, those listening are asked to simply close their eyes and let the words wash over them. The second time, listeners are asked to read along and make notes of any words, phrases, or ideas that stick out to them. The third time, listeners are asked to do the same thing once more: read along and note what stands out. When this time of engaging with the Word is over, you might go right into a reflective song, allowing everyone to continue processing and worshipping God for what was revealed in the reading.

"THE TABLE" THEOLOGY

The table has long held powerful symbolic meaning and connection with community and hospitality, and in the Christian tradition, it is associated with communion. During the Last Supper, Jesus' final meal with his disciples all seated around a table, he invited them to see the ordinary Passover elements of bread and wine in a new light as his body and blood. He says that every time they gathered around a table, eating and drinking together, they were to remember his sacrifice: his body broken and blood poured out for their salvation. Now, more than two thousand years later, we're still upholding Jesus' instructions to gather and partake of these elements around the table together. They remind us of his sacrifice; his triumph over the powers of evil, sin, and death; his eventual return; and his universal invitation to join at the table of mercy where all who respond to the invitation, especially the lowest and the least, will find a seat waiting for them.

The Table can take on many different shapes and forms in the modern-day worship service. It can be the actual table of communion, where we partake of the elements together in remembrance of Jesus, or it can serve a more symbolic role in the service, giving us space to remember, reflect, and process together. Taking communion together in a small group setting can be a little bit difficult and, depending on your denomination, might even be impossible without an elder or ordained minister. For that reason, I'm going to recommend approaching the idea of the Table symbolically—gathering and responding to the Word of God and the workings of the Holy Spirit.

"THE TABLE" APPLICATION

The Table is an important segment of any worship service because it dedicates time for Jesus' followers to reflect and move toward God in response to the love, grace, and instruction they receive from the Word and the Spirit. It's a space where all of God's children are welcome and all are invited to participate; even the act of showing up is appreciated. Though we're engaging with and celebrating the Table symbolically rather than actually partaking in the elements of communion, this time will still retain a similar focus, pointing us toward Christ and each other as we partake in his life and share our lives with each other in prayer and conversation.

This will probably look a little bit different for every group, but the goal is still the same: respond to and remember God's extravagant and invitational love exhibited in Christ. You might choose to do this by asking for prayer requests or testimonies, or by asking if anyone's heart was stirred by Scripture or the Holy Spirit. You could also simply engage in a few moments of silent contemplation. Whatever you choose to do, remember that the communion table—whether literal or symbolic—is both a frighteningly sacred and holy moment and a bafflingly safe and inviting space. Respect it and make room for the Spirit to work and all will be well.

"THE SENDING" THEOLOGY

The final movement of a worship service is the Sending, where God sends the Church back out into the world as Jesus sent the disciples. The Sending is important because it gives us a concrete end to the service and tells us how to re-enter the world as the people of God. Regardless of what happens at this conclusion of the service—whether it's a song, a prayer, or a benediction—the words should carry us out the doors, into the car, down the street, and into our homes and hearts. If the words make it into our homes and our hearts, they might even make it into the homes and hearts of others as well.

"THE SENDING" APPLICATION

The final "Sending" segment for most of the Liturgies in this book includes one final song and a short benediction. For the song, I would recommend something either focusing on God as our Redeemer and Deliverer, or a more missional, outward-facing song. Both are solid options. The participants benefit from a strong end with a song people know and can sing easily; they need to feel familiar and well-connected with at least a couple in your set, and the first and last songs are a great place for those beloved, familiar songs.

The benediction that follows the final song closes the service. You can give a short intro by saying something like, "Now, hear this benediction," or, "Receive this benediction." If you want, you can invite everyone to hold their arms out with open hands facing up in a receiving posture.

In presenting this structure and flow of worship, I hope that you will see it not as the *only* way to organize a worship service, but rather as a tool for you on the journey toward leading engaging, spirit-filled worship. Think of it as a means to an end, with the end being pure, truthful, and Spirit-filled worship. I wholeheartedly believe this approach to worship fosters authentic, Christ-centered worship, but if you find that something else works better, please don't hold back for my sake. Remember, however, that regardless of whether or not you use the Liturgies in this book, your small-group worship will still have its own distinct Liturgy. Even if you just decide to sing some songs and read a passage of Scripture together, that is, in and of itself, a Liturgy, which says a lot about what you value. Don't forego honest, critical self-reflection on your manner and methods of leading worship in smaller settings because your leadership is important, your small group or house church is important, and how you worship together can be life-changing.

CHAPTER THREE

"Oh Captain, My Captain"

Poetry and music are the languages that we humans often use to articulate our deep-felt experiences and emotions. Both often speak in forms only our souls can fully comprehend—beauty, wonder, and truth ringing in our spirits like resonant bells. The most authentic and eternal truths and experiences of life often evade the grasp of everyday syntax and fall flat when described in the most factual, practical, or realistic way. We need the artistic expressions of poetry and melody, especially in worship.

Practical and concise contemporary language is important and necessary, and it makes up a lot of the content of this book, but some subjects and concepts are easier for me to explain with an analogy.

The one that I've found most appropriate and helpful, and which I'll utilize in this chapter, is the analogy of a pilot operating a plane and caring for the passengers. As with any comparison, it doesn't perfectly capture every element, and the deeper you go, the more it breaks down, but the perspective has helped me understand how and why to plan a good worship service.

THE FLIGHT PLAN

Many of the most turbulent moments on a flight occur during take-off and landing. A pilot who does not know how to get the plane off the ground and back again is not one I want to fly with. Similarly, as worship leaders, if we don't know how to get our services off the ground and then eventually land the plane, it's going to be a very bumpy ride.

Worship pilots without a thorough flight plan might be recognizable through a lack of connected emotion in a service. Imagine you're in a church service and just heard a stirring, vulnerable message about lament. The pastor successfully reaches the congregants with powerful moments about ways to mourn with those who are mourning and weeping with those who weep. The church attendees are swept into the memories and contexts that resurface empathy, grief, and exhaustion, many with tears or leaning on their family member's shoulder.

As the pastor gracefully concludes the sermon, the worship leader counts off the drummer into a high-tempo, high-energy, upbeat song of praise. He starts playing his G-major chord and gestures for the others in the room to clap with him.

That kind of emotional whiplash is downright jarring! The aircraft, carefully prepared during the time in the air to reach a safe, peaceful, gentle speed, just fell ten thousand feet in four measures of a worship song. Those passengers just got the wind knocked out of them! They are bonking their heads into the seats in front of them, whimpering and trying to find the flight attendants to ask what just happened. Did the pilot not watch where they were going?

Exiting that plane, many would probably be walking on shaky feet, unsure how to feel now that they are on the ground again. It wasn't a bad *flight*, but certainly a stomach-lurching landing.

The next time, imagine the end of the service is dedicated to a few members of the congregation getting baptized. Each one shares the incredible way that God woo-ed them to his family, and the body of Christ celebrates joyfully as their beloved friends become brothers and sisters. As the pastor pulls each one out of the water, the baptized's face is beaming with relief and awe for everything God has done up to now and will do through them. Their family members wrap them in a clean, white towel and a big, albeit damp hug. They walk back over to their seats with big smiles and full hearts as the worship leader starts playing...a slow, somber hymn. The congregation is led through lyrics reflecting the immense weight of the world, of sin, and weaves in the psalms King David wrote in his darker moments.

The energy from the baptisms is depleted in the song's expectations of lament and exhaustion. Their pilot, who had just flown the passengers through sunny, windless skies, started to panick during the descent, needlessly startling everyone. The passengers thought everything was fine! Was there even danger? Does he see the blue skies out the windows?

Now, obviously, these examples are hyperbolic, but mistakes like this really do happen. Sometimes communication between the pastor and worship leader is lacking, and sometimes worship leaders fail to fully consider what people might feel at a particular moment in the service. When we're leading worship for a small group, a miscommunication-induced mistake like this is less likely because you probably won't be working directly with a pastor.

However, regardless of who is involved, it's always important to consider where God might want to take people emotionally and spiritually, and how we're going to aid the Spirit in helping them arrive. The goal for any worship service, no matter the number of participants, should never be an "emotional high-point." Rather, the goal is to lead people into a space of surrender, shepherding them into the presence of the Holy Spirit by engaging their hearts, minds, and souls. Thankfully, God has given us many tools and safety protocols to build a flight plan that faithfully takes off and lands in the Holy Spirit's presence and the participant's hearts.

Flight Plan Breakdown
THE RUNWAY

After boarding your plane, stowing your luggage, and fastening your seatbelt, you'll hear several messages from the overhead speakers and flight attendants. If you're like me, you probably tune most of these out. If there's one voice you may feel inclined to listen to, it's the voice of the pilot. No matter what the pilot says, the purpose of her or his pre-flight announcement is to welcome passengers, set the expectations for all those on board, and make everyone feel at ease. In many ways, this is also how the greeting and call to worship function in a small-group worship service.

Your words and energy in this welcome and opening piece of liturgy give everyone involved a sense of what is to be expected from this whole experience. Depending on how often you and those you're leading engage with worship in a small group setting, there may be a number of questions rattling around in their minds during the moments that lead up to this time. They might be wondering, "What should I expect for the tone or mood of this experience? Is there a theme for the evening and, if so, what is it? Will this be a more casual and laid-back experience or one that's more serious and intentional?" It's up to you to figure out the answers to some of these questions and implicitly or explicitly express them on the runway *before* take-off.

TAKE-OFF

I almost always have the same thought at some point during every flight: "How on earth is this huge hunk of metal flying through the air at twelve thousand feet above the ground right now?"

Yes, I know that science and the laws of aerodynamics hold the answers to this question, but unfortunately, my one year of college-level physics was not enough to give me a proper understanding. I do, however, know a little bit about Newton's laws of physics—the ones we all learned in high school and forgot as soon as we turned in the test on them—which tell us that it takes exponentially more energy to get an object moving than it does to *keep* it moving afterward. The same could be said in regard to a worship service. The energy required to get your plane off the ground is greater than what is needed to keep it in the air, and that gravity-defying energy will almost always come from the opening song.

It usually takes a lot more energy to get a service moving than it does to keep it going, and if you don't give that worship service enough energy in the right direction from the get-go, you can easily end up off-course or grounded. This means that the songs right after the call to worship, particularly the very first one, are extremely important. For the service to start well, you need to give this song the appropriate amount of energy in the direction you want it to go, whether that's celebration, contemplation, or lament. Turning around is sure to slow you down, so choose these songs wisely! Set your course and rise from the ground confident in the way the service is routed.

TURBULENCE

You're bound to experience turbulence at some point during any flight, and this often happens at take-off. However, every good pilot is prepared for this eventuality and is seldom surprised by a few bumps along the way. The ones who need to be prepared for turbulence are the passengers.

In a worship service, the prayer of confession may be a rather turbulent moment for your average small-group goer. Therefore, it's your job as the leader to prepare them for what's to come and steer the plane safely through these rough pockets of air. As the pilot, you know that these little bumps and drops are normal and nothing to worry about, but to your passengers, they can often be quite scary and unnerving. The best practice is not to avoid turbulence at all costs; if not impossible, this would be very impractical. Our job is to comfort and assure those we're leading that while there may be some jostling and unfamiliar movement ahead, everything will be okay. A good pilot instills trust in their passengers that everything is under control and that they are safe and cared for.

CRUISING

Once cruising altitude is reached, my favorite time-killing activities are reading books and listening to podcasts. I'm a very momentum driven person and sometimes struggle to slow down but know it's something that I desperately need, so I love the fact that plane rides compel me to do so. I often struggle to find (or make) the time to just sit and read for the sake of reading, whether that's reading a great novel, an interesting piece of nonfiction, or even my Bible. I know this is something I struggle with, and I also know for a fact that I'm not the only person in the world dealing with this issue.

Our culture encourages us to constantly fill our time with work and activities we find meaningful, hoping they will fill the void that seems to grow the more we feed it. No one has time to sit down and read anymore, so a moment in worship to simply sit and soak in Scripture can be like a breath of fresh air. There's nowhere to go and nothing to do but quietly sit and listen. Keep this in mind when leading people in a time of engaging with the Word; don't try to make it more than it needs to be. Passengers don't want to hear the pilot talk for the duration of the flight. They just want to be still and enjoy a moment that forcibly slows and quiets all of the monkeys on their backs and in their brains.

STRETCH THOSE LEGS

As a long-legged man, I almost always get up to use the restroom during a flight, even if I don't really need to. It's just the best excuse to move around a little. In this analogy for worship services, the movement I'm referring to is less physical and more relational. People may not stretch their legs, but the hope is that they will stretch their minds and their hearts by reflecting on Scripture and engaging with one another. Just as the pilot needs to turn off the "fasten seatbelt" sign, signaling to passengers that it's okay to move around, you as the worship leader need to provide and facilitate this space for people to move toward God and each other.

People on airplanes are easy to keep tabs on when they're strapped into their seats, but when up and about, there's always a greater chance that something unexpected will happen. People stumble and trip, bumping into each other and waking sleeping babies, all of which are bound to happen as a result of the necessary freedom they're given. Likewise, in this space of movement during small-group worship, we are knowingly adding some potential chaos. You're still flying the plane, but you have a little less control than you might at other moments, and that's okay.

When you give people the opportunity to share what is on their hearts or how the Holy Spirit has moved them during your time together, it's possible that the conversation may not go in the direction that you expected it to go, and that's okay! Part of being a good pilot, host, and worship leader entails being flexible enough that people can bring their whole messy and beautiful selves to the table. Trust that with a little guidance and time, everyone will return and "refasten their seatbelts" a little happier and healthier than before.

DROPS

Occasionally on flights, especially in less-than-ideal weather, strong winds will make the plane shake rather violently, or even imitate the feeling of the plane dropping out from under you for a moment. Even the best pilots can't always be perfectly prepared for these situations, but knowing what to do if this occurs is crucial for the safety and well-being of your passengers. This is never a fun moment, but it does happen occasionally in worship, and being prepared for it as the leader is the best way to recover.

If something ever does go horribly awry and you wish to live out the rest of your days as a hermit, never showing your face in public again, first of all, don't panic. More likely than not, whatever happened is much, much less obvious to the people you're leading than it is to you. Whether you played a bad chord, sang the wrong words, or had an embarrassing pre-pubescent voice crack (definitely *not* speaking from experience), never completely stop or pause. As much as you can, just pick up where you left off and keep going.

If you're one of those few people blessed with good humor and a below-average level of insecurity, it can sometimes be appropriate to take a moment and laugh at yourself for your silly mistake, particularly if it's something that will make finishing the song difficult, like starting in the wrong key. Most of the time, however, if you play a wrong, nasty-sounding chord, or sing the wrong words, just keep on keeping on. Hopefully, at the end of the day, people are more focused on worshipping God than on you and your mistakes.

LANDING

Now, as we reach the end of our flight, it's time to begin the descent and land the plane. Just like take-off, the landing is important because the plane needs to slow down at the right speed in the correct amount of time to hit the landing strip safely and stop in time.

As the first song got you into the air at the beginning, so the last song will steer you back to solid ground now. Let's first make sure we understand what "the ground" actually is. What is *grounding* this time of worship? If it's an idea or a theme (e.g., expectation in the Advent season), then it's best to return to that idea or theme as you make your way back to the ground. The closing song needs to have enough energy to keep the plane from nose-diving out of the sky, still moving at a good speed to lower itself incrementally. Of course, we also don't want to stimulate so much energy that the plane overshoots the landing strip, launching into a 30 minute encore (unless that's where the Spirit takes you). Remember, a perfect landing is rare, but one that doesn't slam to the ground and cause people to "death-grip" their armrest is generally a success.

TAXIING

You made it safely to the ground! Well done! The hard work is over. Now we simply need to thank the passengers for flying on the airline and help them prepare to exit the plane for the next leg of their journey.

It may be tempting to think that these final words hold little significance, but these are your parting words to them as they go out into the great unknown beyond the exit light. Sure, some might be tuning out, but these departing words are important. As a worship leader, never underestimate the power of a good benediction. Oftentimes what we remember best from an experience is not what happens in the middle but at the beginning and the end. These final statements and acknowledgments may be the words that remain in their minds more clearly than any others, so make sure they count.

Leading small group worship—like piloting an airplane—is hardly a walk in the park, and while a real pilot might be able to engage "autopilot" at some point, you don't have that luxury. Why? Because (surprise) you're not actually the pilot. You, my friend, are the co-pilot, and as the co-pilot, you must be constantly focused and engaged, paying close attention to all the numbers, meters, and flashing lights on your dashboard that tell you what's going on around you. Worship leaders are really *less* than half of what's guiding this experience. The real pilot, the Holy Spirit, must be the one calling the shots. Without the Spirit, this plane has no chance of even getting off the ground, much less making it back safely. However, you still have an important job as the co-pilot, and a lot of responsibility lies in your hands, which can feel burdensome.

So remember to take a moment and pause.

Take a deep breath. Remember that at the end of the day, no matter how well or poorly things seem to be going, our Perfect Pilot always flies the plane exactly where it needs to go.

CHAPTER FOUR

Diversity

One of the most beautiful and challenging aspects of a healthy church or small group is the diversity of its body. Looking at Scripture, it's apparent that God's dream for the Church is a people who are unified but not uniform—the more threads in the tapestry or tiles in the mosaic of the Church, the more complete our reflection of God will be. The challenge of diversity, however, lies in our ineptitude for seeing, understanding, and welcoming experiences and perspectives different from our own. There's no way around this fact; it's just downright challenging to live in a community with people who look, act, feel, and think differently from us, whether that's politically, culturally, economically, or theologically. Only Christlike love and humility through the Holy Spirit in us can bring such a vast array of people together under one roof and, even then, we'll never get along perfectly. Leading worship for a diverse group of people is difficult but there is much to be gained by leaning into the challenges it may bring.

I was born and raised in small-town Arkansas, in a cluster of cities nestled comfortably between great wealth and extreme poverty. Economic diversity—or "disparity" might be a better word—is abundant in this part of the state, with elite CEOs from one of the world's largest and wealthiest corporations (Wal-Mart) making their beds just a few miles from folks who barely have roofs over their heads. There's a good amount of racial and cultural diversity in Northwest Arkansas (NWA) as well. Many Latin American families live and work in the community, and many South Asian families are transplanted there after being hired by Wal-Mart's enormous technology department. The cul-de-sac I grew up in was home to multiple Indian families, many with children who were my childhood friends for many years.

Northwest Arkansas is a surprisingly diverse area, yet like much of the South, it bears the scars of prejudice and racism that mar its history and still affect its present. I knew this long before coming to understand some of the complex ins and outs of racism because of one obvious fact: there were no Black people in NWA. I'm exaggerating a bit but, truthfully, very few African-American folks lived in NWA during my childhood. The reason is disturbingly simple. When my parents were children, just one generation ago, the Ku Klux Klan was still running Black families out through discriminatory policies, hostility, and violence. For this reason (and other subsequent reasons), I didn't have any Black friends growing up. In fact, I can't honestly say I had a Black friend until I was nineteen or twenty years old.

Moving to Richmond, Virginia and joining a racially diverse church in 2019 was life-changing, but because of my whitewashed suburban childhood, it was also challenging. I had to learn a lot about the new space I'd recently entered, and consequently made a lot of mistakes along the way. One of the most humorous and embarrassing blunders I made was in asking a woman of color and new friend of mine about her hair. I had recently learned about some of the ways that Black women style their hair, and I genuinely liked and was curious about hers. This new friend of mine very graciously told me that I should never ask a Black woman whether her hair is a weave or a wig, and while I was incredibly embarrassed at my mistake, I'm also very grateful that she chose to kindly correct me. I would never have learned how to be a good friend and neighbor to the Black women in my community without interactions like that.

I've learned much more from my Black sisters and brothers in Christ here in Richmond than I will ever be able to teach them. That said, I'm committed to investing everything I can into this multiethnic, intergenerational small group my wife and I call home, and a big part of that has been realized through worship.

Leading worship effectively for this diverse group meant first observing and learning about this community's style and habits of worship, which were different from those with which I grew up. This group, like every longstanding group of people, had and still has a unique history and culture shaped by its past experiences. While I absolutely brought my own style and ideas into the planning and execution of worship, there's still a balance—a give and take—between my paradigm for small-group worship and the pre-existing culture of the group. I introduced the Five Pillars of Worship (Gathering, Responding, Word, Table, Sending) and established a more regular practice of corporate confession while simultaneously learning and playing songs that were unfamiliar to me but well-loved by the group.

If you find yourself leading worship in a diverse setting, whether that's a diversity of age, race, or ideology, you will likely find yourself in a very similar situation. However, with the pre-designed Liturgies in this book, all you really have to worry about are the music and Bible passages. When it comes to thoughtfully selecting songs for a diverse group of people, I have two pieces of advice: first, use songs that are sung frequently at the church you all attend. If you're unsure exactly which songs fall into your church's "canon," reach out to your worship pastor or music director and most will be happy to send you a list of regularly played songs. Second, talk to the people in your small group or house church. Ask them which songs they most connect with and enjoy singing. You can do this in person (face to face), or you can do it virtually, over text, or with something like a group poll online.

Adapting to and leading a diverse group of people takes a lot of work and patience. No matter who you are or what range of diversity is present in your group, you will always have some learning to do. We all have blind spots and presuppositions created by our cultural influences, so don't be dismayed if you find that you made an incorrect assumption. You might assume that everyone will remain seated throughout worship, that everyone loves long, Spirit-led songs, or that no one will burst out into spontaneous prayer. Whatever the assumption is, if and when it's shattered, remember you're not a failure. Perhaps you were uneducated or short-sighted in how a different culture worships, but a mistake only becomes a failure if you don't take the opportunity to learn and grow from the experience. Spend time with people who aren't like you, find out what helps them connect with God during worship, and ask if there are specific postures or elements of worship that feel especially important to them.

Engaging in diverse spaces requires honesty, humility, and patience, and good practices among diverse groups of people always boil down to hospitality. It's easy to be welcoming and hospitable to people who are like us, but we can be inadvertently inhospitable to those who are different. We quickly assume that everyone will enjoy and connect with exactly what we enjoy and connect with, and that's just not always the case. Good hospitality requires an element of denying ourselves in order to meet the needs and desires of people who want and need differently than we do. You may not feel comfortable or familiar with a specific song, but if you know that people with different backgrounds and experiences find joy and meaningful connection with God through it and it's theologically sound, it's your responsibility to strongly consider playing it, regardless of how you feel personally.

As a general rule of thumb for worship in a *diverse space*, remember this: if you are comfortable more than seventy-five percent of the time, your cultural expression is too dominant, and that comfort probably comes at the expense of others in the group. However, remember that this rule only applies to truly diverse spaces. If the group that you are leading is less diverse or, perhaps, not diverse at all, that changes the accuracy of this rule. However, it can still be benificial to introduce your community to culturally diverse music! A lack of diversity is never something to be ashamed of, but I do believe that diversity is always something that we should strive towards. Not as a means of virtue signaling, but because the body of Christ tends to become a bit lop-sided if everyone looks, thinks, and acts just like everyone else.

In small-group worship, this level of familial hospitality—making people feel like members of the family—is so important for fostering an unconditionally warm and welcoming ethos. Ask questions, don't make assumptions, listen to what others have to say, and above all, put the needs and wants of others over and above your own. *Then* you will create a space where all kinds of diversity have the space to thrive.

CHAPTER FIVE

Leading with Others

At my first job in Richmond and first "real job" out of college, I worked as the worship leader for a small church plant in the suburbs of Richmond called Community West. By this point in my life, I had been leading worship for six or seven years, and until then had worked more or less autonomously. For better or worse, I was always the one picking the songs, building the band, and writing the prayers on my own. However, this was not entirely the case at Community West.

The songs I selected and the prayers I wrote were all looked over and commented on by the lead pastor two weeks before being implemented. He generally liked the prayers I wrote and the songs I selected, but also frequently offered suggestions, ideas, and pushback, which was quite foreign to me—I wasn't used to being questioned or offered suggestions as a worship leader. Initially, this experience did cause me to bristle a bit, but in no time at all, I realized that collaboration almost always made my prayers and song selections stronger and better suited for our congregation.

Collaboration tends to be difficult because we're letting go of power and control. No two minds operate exactly the same, so teamwork takes communication skills, patience, and understanding. The result of that compromise and release of control is a greater depth of creativity and meaningful discussion. To truly imitate God is to let go of power and bring others into the work of "creating," just as God welcomed us from the very beginning by inviting Adam to name the animals.

Still, as we see in Genesis, when you let go of control things may not go exactly as you had planned. They may even go quite awry! Disagreements, arguments, misunderstandings, and hurt feelings are all possible when you collaborate. Love, however, prompts us to believe that even the possibility of those difficulties is worth the risk because love always welcomes, always surrenders power to others, and always humbly realizes that greater good will come from working together than from working alone.

The task of collaboration really boils down to humility—limitations can be a gift. Collaboration is an opportunity to be grateful for the talents and skills of others, and when you aren't pitted in competition against one another, it creates a beautiful opportunity for growth and excellence. So, how do we submit ourselves to this kind of humble collaboration in these small group worship spaces?

First, you need to think about where and how to invite others into the process of planning a worship service.

This requires self-examination; that is, asking the hard but beneficial question: "Where am I inadequate?"

Am I inadequate in selecting songs that will resonate with this community? Am I inadequate in selecting the right passage of Scripture, or in leading people to engage with it? There are probably many places where the talent, wisdom, and insights of others would be valuable, so my advice is to start by just picking one. Say, for instance, you're not very good at playing the guitar, but you know that Maria So-and-So is quite talented. You could try to lead and play yourself, but you know that Maria would do a much better job, and you know that with her help, you would have much more attention to focus on other aspects of leading.

You reach out to Maria, who is thrilled to help out and play guitar, so you send her the setlist of the songs you want to play and what prayers and Scripture you're planning to use. To your surprise, Maria is quite opinionated and interjects her own thoughts about which songs, prayers, and passages might suit the service well.

In this hypothetical situation, the initial decision to ask Maria took a certain level of humility—asking and trusting someone else to take on this instrumental role. However, truly honoring the collaborative process requires inviting the other person involved to jump in and fully mess with the sand in the creative sandbox. This doesn't mean they're allowed to come in and kick over all that you've built, but it does mean that space must be made for their whole self, including all of the thoughts and opinions that come with them. These thoughts and opinions do not always need to be implemented—pushback is often warranted—but they must at least be fully heard and considered. Maria may have some excellent suggestions and some mediocre suggestions. Your job is to humbly accept the good suggestions and kindly and confidently discern, discuss, and speak of your opinions on those that you disagree with. Good collaborative teams are able to find the rhythm and balance of this.

Here, I think it is important to state that humility is different from self-deprecation. Self-deprecation leads us to doubt our own skills, abilities, and expertise. In a self-deprecating attitude, we defer to others because we're afraid of trusting ourselves. Humility, on the other hand, leads us to acknowledge our own talent and wisdom while convicting us that the market is never cornered. Humility reminds us that others may have just as much, if not more, talent, wisdom, and expertise in an area as we do ourselves. If we doubt our own abilities and expertise, the community will not gain from what we have to offer. If, however, we engage with humility that acknowledges both our talents and shortcomings, we will find that what was impossible on our own becomes not only possible but beautifully realized in partnering with another human soul.

It may not always be the case that you collaborate with someone who is filled with thoughts and ideas and is unafraid to share them. You will find that some people are genuinely happy to go with the flow and glad just to participate. Others may have some thoughts and ideas but not feel the confidence or liberty to share them either because of inexperience, self-doubt, or another, unknown reason. As the leader and individual with power and control in this situation, you have to figure out how much of that control you are going to give to the person you decided to collaborate with, and the answer may not always be as easy as a fifty-fifty split. Sometimes it may be wise to give more, and other times, less. If the person you're collaborating with is eager but less experienced, it might be wise to share a little less power until they have the skill and experience to use it wisely. On the other hand, if the person is more skilled and experienced than you are, you might want to hand over more and let them give you an abundance of direction and insight.

If this idea of collaboration around planning and executing a worship service is new and a bit foreign to you, here are some practical tips and ideas about how to start bringing others into the process:

First, consider the other leaders in your small group or house church or, if you are the only leader, those in your group who occupy leadership positions outside of the group. Ask them for ideas and insights about which songs may be best for your group, or what songs might fit best with a certain theme.

Ask them to weigh in on which Bible verses to use or even logistical topics, like when and where to host a worship night for your group.

You can also ask someone to lead a prayer during the service. Ask them to write it out beforehand if you're unsure about their experience with public speaking and praying—there's no shame in reading a written prayer that you thoughtfully crafted ahead of time.

Creative and logistical collaboration takes practice, and it can often seem like everything would be a lot faster and easier if you just did it yourself. That might be true! Sometimes that might be all that you have the time and energy to accomplish. But I know from experience that collaboration is important because it gives our creative endeavors life, light, and energy in ways that we can never achieve on our own. It's not all about us. We are truly more than the sum of our parts, and we are most like our Creator not when we hold all of the power and control, but when we invite and welcome others into the dance of collaborative creativity.

Using the Liturgies

Planning a whole worship set, especially for a small group event, can be stressful, tedious, and time-consuming, even for someone with years of experience and a degree in ministry. The twelve Liturgies you will find in the following pages are purposefully designed to make this process of planning and leading small-group worship easy, intentional, and life-giving both for you and those you're leading.

You'll find three objectives on the title page of every Liturgy outlining what it can help you accomplish on both theological and formational levels. These aren't meant to be goals that you check off a list after leading but simply guides to provide direction and understanding. In the same vein, I offer three passages of Scripture on the title page that correlate. Most Liturgies will have one passage from the Old Testament, one from the Gospels, and one from the epistles (letters). Feel free to use any combination of these or something different entirely.

Another laborious component of preparing to lead worship is drafting a guide with lyrics, Bible verses, and prayers. I've got you! Simply visit https://haydenhobby95.wixsite.com/hayden-hobby to access digital, printable templates of all twelve Liturgies, and you can insert your own song lyrics and Scripture in it too. Hopefully this will save you some time formatting!

This book is designed to work for you so that you can work less. So let it do the work and lean into what you do best: helping people engage with a loving and holy God through worship.

LITURGIES

IN THE NAME OF THE SOURCE

LORD, our Lord,
how majestic is your name in all the earth!

You have set your glory
in the heavens.
Through the praise of children and infants
you have established a stronghold against your enemies,
to silence the foe and the avenger.
When I consider your heavens,
the work of your fingers,
the moon and the stars,
which you have set in place,
what is mankind that you are mindful of them,
human beings that you care for them?

LORD, our Lord,
how majestic is your name in all the earth!

Psalm 8:1-4, 9 (NIV)

A Liturgy on (re)Creation

Objectives:

1. To invite God's Spirit to renew and re-create us.
2. To better understand what it means to be made new.
3. To spark our desire to join God's work of transformation in the world.

Scripture:

1. Genesis 1 or 2
2. John 3:1-8
3. 2 Corinthians 5:11-21

Call to Worship

Leader
In the beginning was the Creator God,
who spoke and sang and laughed
the universe into existence,
filling the emptiness with love and
the darkness with light.

People
Creator God, fill our emptiness with your love,
and flood our darkness with your light.

Leader
In the beginning, the Creator gave order to the chaos
and meaning to all of creation,
assigning days to mark the seasons,
and seasons to mark the years, giving roles and a purpose
to every plant and animal under the sun.

People
Creator God, bring order to our chaos
and purpose to all that we do, think, and say.

Leader
In the beginning, the Spirit of the Creator
entered the human beings created in his likeness,
filling them with hope, joy, love, and peace,
patience, kindness, goodness,
gentleness, and self-control.

All

Spirit of God, fill us and transform us
to be the humans we were created to be, amen.

Prayer

(That God would fill us with the spirit of renewal and life.)

Song #1

"_____" by _____.

upbeat, focused on the theme, familiar

Song #2

"_____" by _____.

more contemplative, medium energy

Corporate Prayer of Confession

Leader

Lord Jesus, we come before you
to confess our need to be renewed and re-created.
With every breath in, we need your life-giving Spirit
to gather up the darkness within us.
Expel our brokenness and sin with every breath out

to make room for your goodness and light.

All

Create in us clean hearts, oh God,
and renew your Holy Spirit within us.

Leader

We confess, also, to our frequent fear of your offer
to make us into a new creation.
While we long to be healed and made whole,
we're afraid of losing ourselves
in the process of renewal—
scared of being washed away while being
washed clean in the blood of the Lamb.

All

Create in us clean hearts, oh God,
and renew your Holy Spirit within us.

Leader

Forgive us for clinging so tightly
to the jagged edges of our broken vessels, oh Lord,
and remind us that the old self,
crucified when we are made new,
was never our true self to begin with.
Empower us to release the fragments that
wound ourselves and those we love.

All

Create in us clean hearts, oh God,
and renew your Holy Spirit within us.

Reading from Scripture

(Pause for a few moments to hear from Scripture together)

Song #3

"_____" by _____.

reflective, introspective, lower energy

Response to the Word

(Pause for a few moments to hear from others in the group)

Song #4

"_____" by _____.

focus on God as Redeemer and Deliverer, medium-building energy

Benediction
May the Spirit of our Lord Jesus Christ
go with you as a blessing,
comfort, conviction, and a charge:
to always fight for justice,
pray for healing,
and listen for God.

A Liturgy on Justice

Objectives:

1. To awaken our hearts to the need for justice in our communities.
2. To acknowledge and repent from our inaction toward injustice.
3. To lament the injustice in our community, nation, and world.

Scripture:

1. Isaiah 58
2. Luke 18:1-8
3. James 2:14-25

Call to Worship

Leader

In the fullness of your kingdom, Oh Lord,
all things will be made right.
You have called us to share in your good work
to free the oppressed and break every chain that binds.

People

Let your justice roll like a river,
your righteousness like a mighty stream!

Leader

You have called us to love righteousness and justice,
to care for the poor and the widow,
and to feed the hungry and clothe the naked.
You call us to love our neighbor even unto death.

People

Let your justice roll like a river,
your righteousness like a mighty stream!

Leader

You are a God of justice and grace,
loving the sinner and the saint,
and we praise you for the grace you offer
and the justice you demand.

All

Let us praise the Lord whose justice rolls like a river
and whose grace overflows like a fountain.

Prayer

(That God would work through us to bring freedom from physical and spiritual oppression.)

Song #1

" _____ " by _____.

upbeat, focused on the theme, familiar

Song #2

" _____ " by _____.

more contemplative, medium energy

Corporate Prayer of Confession

Leader
Gracious God, we confess to our sinful sleep
in light of the injustice in our community.
In our comfortable complacency,
we often lack the motivation
to arise and see our neighbors in need.

All
Forgive us for our complacency toward injustice.

Leader
Justice requires discomfort, sacrifice, and risk.

We confess that on most days, we are not willing
to make the sacrifice or take the risk
that true justice requires.

All
Forgive us for our complacency toward injustice.

Leader
We claim to know you and walk in your ways,
talking as those who love the least of these,
but what do our hands say—are we holding up
the ones who cannot stand on their own?
What do our feet say—are we moving toward
the poor and the marginalized?

All
Forgive us for our complacency towards injustice.

Leader:
While we may have been asleep
to the injustice all around us,
we serve a God who forgives and redeems.
By the power of the Spirit,
we trust that God will wake us,
remake us, and turn our hearts of stone
into hearts of flesh,
ready and willing to join
in the kingdom work of justice, amen.

Song #3

"_____" by _____.

reflective, introspective, lower energy

Reading from Scripture

Song #4

"_____" by _____.

connects with the passage of Scripture, medium energy

Response to the Word

Song #5

"_____" by _____.

focus on God as Redeemer and Deliverer, medium-building energy

Benediction
May the Spirit of our Lord Jesus Christ
go with you as a blessing,
comfort, conviction, and a charge:
to always fight for justice,
pray for healing,
and listen for God.

A Liturgy on God as Mother

Objectives:

1. To expand our perspective on God's true nature.
2. To lift up and encourage our mothers, sisters, and daughters in Christ.
3. To help us see the feminine image of God in others.

Scripture:

1. Isaiah 49:8-16
2. Psalm 91:1-8
3. Luke 13:31-35

Call to Worship

Leader
As an eager child leaps into the arms of their mother,
we now fall into the warmth of your embrace, Oh Lord.

People
Here we find safety, love, and acceptance

Leader
For who but a mother would love us so selflessly?
Saying *"This is my body broken for you,"*
and *"This is my body, take and eat."*

People
Christ, like a mother, has done this for us.

Leader
Nurturing and protecting, giving life, love,
and meaning to her beloved children.

All
That we all might grow into the fullness of her image,
the image of Christ, amen.

Prayer

*(Asking God to open our eyes that we might see her with a
new perspective.)*

Song #1

" _____ " by _____.

upbeat, focused on the theme, familiar

Song #2

" _____ " by _____.

more contemplative, medium energy

Corporate Prayer of Confession

Leader

Mother God, we confess that throughout time,
we have failed to acknowledge
and consider your feminine nature,
seeing only one half of the image we are created in.

All

Forgive us for overlooking your motherly nature, oh Lord.

Leader

Whether father or mother, your title
does not change your character or nature Lord,
but our damagingly low view of the feminine has hurt us all,
stunting our ability to fully see and accept
the broad spectrum of your love and grace.

All

Forgive us for overlooking your motherly nature,
oh Lord.

Leader

But thanks be to God, sisters and brothers,
that through the life, death, and resurrection of Jesus Christ,
we have been forgiven of our sins, reconciled to God,
and shown a true and perfect example of fatherhood
and motherhood, amen.

Song #3

"_____" by _____.

reflective, introspective, lower energy

Reading from Scripture

(Depending on which passage(s) of Scripture you read
and your group's level of openness, you might consider
exchanging the "he" pronouns used for God with "her,"
particularly in the Old Testament. While God is always
referred to as male in Scripture, we know that God is
mysteriously both male and female because both were
created in God's image. If you choose to do this, make
sure to explain it to your group beforehand.)

Song #4

"_____" by _____.

connects with the passage of Scripture, medium energy

Response to the Word

Song #5

"_____" by _____.

focus on God as Redeemer and Deliverer, medium-building energy

Benediction
May the peace of our Lord Jesus Christ
Go with you as a blessing,
Comfort, conviction, and a charge:
to always fight for justice,
pray for healing,
and listen for God.

A Liturgy on God as Healer

Objectives:

1. To expand our reliance on the holistic healing of God.
2. To bring what needs to be healed in our lives before God.
3. To engage with the healing of our community alongside God.

Scripture:

1. Numbers 21:4-8
2. John 9:1-12
3. Revelation 22:1-5

Call to Worship

Leader

Amazing grace, how sweet the sound,
that saved our lifeless souls.

People

What once was lost has now been found,
and what was dead has come to life.

Leader

You have replaced our hearts of stone with hearts of flesh,
and our blind eyes and deaf ears have been opened.

People

So that we might perceive your once-invisible kingdom
here in our midst.

Leader

Come, let us worship the Lord!

All

For by his grace we are saved, and in his scars, we are healed.

Prayer

(Praising Jesus as Healer/asking that he heal our world and community.)

Song #1

"_____" by _____.

upbeat, focused on the theme, familiar

Song #2

"_____" by _____.

more contemplative, medium energy

Corporate Prayer of Confession

Leader
Gracious and loving God,
we come before you today
acknowledging our shortcomings
and all the ways we have failed
to reflect you and your kingdom.
Instead, our brokenness is reflected
in our neighborhood, our country, and our world.

It's reflected in our vision of and care for the earth
and all that you created.
For so long we have failed to uphold your charge
to love our kindred creation as good and tender gardeners
and instead, we take, use, and abuse
all that your creation has to offer.

All

Forgive us for contributing to the brokenness of the earth.

Leader

Our brokenness is reflected in our lack of engagement
with the systems and politics of this country.
During seasons of political and civil tension,
we are rarely slow to speak or get angry,
but instead, see the world through ego-induced blinders
that make an enemy of all who disagree.

All

Forgive us for contributing to the brokenness of our nation.

Leader

It is also reflected in how we care
for our neighborhood and community.
So many among us are hurting, impoverished,
addicted, and depressed,
and while you, O Lord, ask us to feed the hungry
and clothe the naked,
it's often easier to just look the other way.

All

Forgive us for contributing
to the brokenness of our neighborhood.

Leader

But thanks be to God that even in our brokenness,
we do not hinder the coming of your kingdom, Lord Jesus.
In your life, death, and resurrection, we are freed to live

fully into your plans to save,
restore, and reconcile this broken and loved world, amen.

Song #3

"_____" by _____.

reflective, introspective, lower energy

Reading from Scripture

Song #4

"_____" by _____.

connects with the passage of Scripture, medium energy

Response to the Word

Song #5

"_____" by _____.

focus on God as Redeemer and Deliverer, medium-building energy

Benediction

May the peace of our Lord Jesus Christ
go with you as a blessing,
comfort, conviction, and a charge:
to always fight for justice,
pray for healing,
and listen for God.

LITURGIES

IN THE NAME OF THE WORD

*"From the beginning of time, God has spoken
life and breath into all of creation. That Word of Life spoken
was with God and was God from the very beginning.
Through this Living Word, all things were created; without him,
nothing would exist. The Word of Life is a light seen shining
through the eyes of all humankind and the darkness
has not yet fully overcome it.*

*There was a man sent by God named John
who proclaimed the truth of the light, calling all to believe.
This man was not the light but a witness to it. The true light
and life-giving breath—pumping God's likeness into all
human beings—
would soon walk the earth.*

*The world, however, would not recognize its Creator;
the one who made all things would not be received
by that which he had made. Yet, to all who did accept and trust
him as Savior, he gave the authority of God as their true Father,
through whom they would be reborn as the holy children of God.*

*The Word of Life came from the Father to live
among us as a man with skin and bones and flesh, and we
have seen his glory as the only Son of God, showing grace
and speaking the truth. The grace that we receive
from his abundance
comes in place of that which we were already given by Moses.
No one except the Son, the Word of Life, has ever truly seen God,
but being God himself, he has made God known to us."*

(Poetic Paraphrase of John 1:1-14)

A Liturgy on Radical Hospitality

Objectives:

1. To reorient our understanding of inclusion and hospitality.
2. To catch Jesus' radical vision of welcoming strangers and outcasts.
3. To begin seeing those on the margins and invite them into Christian community.

Scripture:

1. Genesis 18:1-7
2. Matthew 25:31-40
3. Luke 14:15-24

Call to Worship

Leader
Come, take your seat beside the weak and the powerful,
the poor and the rich.

People
For all are welcome
at the table of the Lamb.

Leader
Take off your shoes, wash the feet of your enemy,
and be washed by the hands of those you have wronged.

People
For all are welcome
at the table of the Lamb.

Leader
Feast and lift your voices to the Lord
beside the downtrodden and afflicted,
the immigrant and weary traveler.

All
For all are welcome at the table of the Lamb,
and here, all find life and rest.

Prayer

(Pray that all would feel welcomed, that this space would be hospitable and inviting.)

Song #1

" _____ " by _____.

upbeat, focused on the theme, familiar

Song #2

" _____ " by _____.

more contemplative, medium energy

Prayer of Confession

Leader
Gracious God,
we come before you now
to confess that we have sinned against you
in our thoughts, words, and deeds—
by what we have done,
and what we have left undone.

Lord, we know that you desire the salvation of every person,
that all people would accept the gracious gift of your love,

but we confess that sometimes our desires
are not in line with yours.
Often, rather than inviting people into the light
of your love and grace,
we condemn them with our crooked standards
and slap them with our faulty rulers.

All
Forgive us for excluding our neighbors
from the good news of your grace.

Leader
You have invited all who are willing to sit at your table,
excluding none on the basis of class, gender, age, or race.
Yet, we continually act as those James spoke of,
who judge others with evil thoughts,
offering a seat of honor to the rich
but telling the poor to sit at our feet.

All
Forgive us for excluding our neighbors
from the good news of your grace.

Leader
In our zeal for righteousness,
we often forget that you alone are good, O Lord,
and as a result, we create a false gospel of conditional love
which excludes people who don't look like us,
think like us, or live like us.
The invitations of your love and mercy

are as deep and wide as the sea,
but in our brokenness, we limit them
to fit our own small view of your work of salvation.

All

Forgive us for excluding our neighbors
from the good news of your grace.

Leader

But thanks be to God that in the wideness of your mercy,
you continually extend your grace
and the offer of salvation to all people,
forgiving us for our shortcomings and the ways we wrong you,
others, and ourselves. Amen.

Song #3

" _____ " by _____.

reflective, introspective, lower energy

Reading from Scripture

Song #4

" _____ " by _____.

connects with the passage of Scripture, medium energy

Response to the Word

Song #5

"_____" by _____.

focus on God as Redeemer and Deliverer, medium-building energy

Benediction
May the Spirit of our Lord Jesus Christ
go with you as a blessing,
comfort, conviction, and a charge:
to always fight for justice,
pray for healing,
and listen for God.

A Liturgy on Reconciliation

Objectives:

1. To come to terms with our need for reconciliation with God and others.
2. To know and understand God's work of reconciliation through Jesus.
3. To become agents of reconciliation in our community.

Scripture:

1. Genesis 45:1-18
2. Luke 19
3. Romans 5:1-11

Call to Worship

Leader
Gracious God, we praise you this morning
because you never stop making a way
for us to find reconciliation.
Through both the goodness
and the brokenness of humanity,
you have always cleared the pathway to help us
heal our tattered relationship with you and with each other.
We see that through the foolishness and faithfulness of
Abraham and Sarah...

People
You made a way.

Leader
Through the folly and the wisdom of Joseph...

People
You made a way.

Leader
Through the deceit and courage of Rehab...

People
You made a way.

Leader
Through the warnings and the rebukes of the prophets
and the judges...

People

You made a way.

Leader

And once and for all, through the life, death,
and resurrection of your son, Jesus Christ…

People

You made a way.

Leader

A way for us all to find healing and reconciliation
in our homes, our neighborhoods,
our nation, and with you.

All

So we lift up our voices in praise to the Lord, for Jesus
has made us a way!

Prayer

*(Asking God to bring about reconciliation in our
community.)*

Song #1

" _____ " by _____.

upbeat, focused on the theme, familiar

"_____" by _____.

more contemplative, medium energy

Corporate Prayer of Confession

Leader

Gracious God,
we come before you now to confess
that we have sinned against you
in our thoughts, words, and deeds—
by what we have done and what we have left undone.

We confess that regardless of ethnicity, race, or creed,
we often fail to wholeheartedly strive for reconciliation
with the strangers and foreigners in our lives—
the men and women we perceive as a danger
to our way of life.

All

Forgive us for putting our own self-interest before
reconciliation with our neighbor.

Leader

If we *are* those with cultural privilege, Lord,
we confess that like Zacchaeus, we have played a part
in the oppression and marginalization
of your beloved children.

Known or unbeknownst to us, we are complicit in the systems
that exploit and take advantage of our brothers and sisters.

All
Forgive us for putting our own self-interest
before seeking justice for and reconciliation
with our neighbor.

Leader
If we *are not* those with cultural privileges, Lord,
we confess that like Jonah, we often run far and fast
from the idea of forgiving those who have wronged us.
We would often rather see your fiery justice rain down
than see evildoers repent and be saved.

All
Forgive us for putting our own self-interest before
forgiveness
and reconciliation with our neighbor.

Leader
But thanks be to God
that no matter who we are or where we're at
on the path toward justice and reconciliation,
we love and serve a just and forgiving God.
A God who not only wants to reconcile us with each other
but a God who has already fully reconciled us to himself
through the atoning life, death,
and resurrection of his son, Jesus Christ,
to whom belongs all glory and honor, forever and ever,
amen.

Song #3

" _____ " by _____.

reflective, introspective, lower energy

Reading from Scripture

Song #4

" _____ " by _____.

connects with the passage of Scripture, medium energy

Response to the Word

Song #5

" _____ " by _____.

focus on God as Redeemer and Deliverer, medium–building energy

Benediction

May the peace of our Lord Jesus Christ
go with you as a blessing,
comfort, conviction, and a charge:
to always fight for justice,
pray for healing,
and listen for God.

A Liturgy Against Condemnation

Objectives:

1. To free ourselves from the weight of perceived condemnation from God.
2. To retrain ourselves to stop judging and condemning others for their sins.
3. To live in the freedom of God's abundant grace and forgiveness.

Scripture:

1. Jonah 3; 4:1-4
2. John 8:1-11
3. Romans 8:1-4

Call to Worship

Leader
Come, let us celebrate the good news
that we have been saved from death
and made alive in Christ!

People
The sin that once condemned us to death has been
stripped of its power.

Leader
Because Jesus was condemned and put to death
by the fullness of sin and evil,
but in his last moments, he cried out,

People
"Father, forgive them!"

Leader
At the cross, the vilest sin was forgiven,
and in the resurrection, the greatest evil was defeated.

People
For this reason, we will worship and follow the Lord!

All
The God who freely forgives even the greatest of sins.

Prayer

(Thanking God for his grace and forgiveness.)

Song #1

"_____" by _____.

upbeat, focused on the theme, familiar

Song #2

"_____" by _____.

more contemplative, medium energy

Corporate Prayer of Confession

Leader
Lord, you have told us that pride comes before the fall.

All
And how great a fall ours has been.

Leader
Since the dawn of time we have fallen...

All

Thinking that we can judge good from evil,
right from wrong.

Leader

In our pride, we have continued to act as God…

All

Judging our neighbors and condemning their actions.

Leader

But the only ones we condemn are ourselves…

All

And the judgment forced on our neighbor
exposes our foolish pride.

Leader

But thanks be to God that in Christ,
there is no condemnation—
only forgiveness, humility, and grace.
And in him, we are free to love
and accept others and ourselves.

Song #3

" _____ " by _____ .

reflective, introspective, lower energy

Reading from Scripture

Song #4

" _____ " by _____ .

connects with the passage of Scripture, medium energy

Response to the Word

Song #5

" _____ " by _____ .

focus on God as Redeemer and Deliverer, medium- to low-building energy

Benediction
May the peace of our Lord Jesus Christ
go with you as a blessing,
comfort, conviction, and a charge:
to always fight for justice,
pray for healing,
and listen for God.

A Liturgy on Jesus as King

Objectives:

1. To grow our sense of allegiance to the kingdom and Lordship of Jesus.
2. To illustrate Jesus' subversive and unexpected methods of authority and leadership.
3. To expose and be rid of persons or places of allegiance higher than Jesus.

Scripture:

1. Daniel 7:9-14
2. Luke 19:28-40
3. Ephesians 1:15-23

Call to Worship

Leader

See, he comes not as a warrior or general,
but as a servant, humble and lowly,
riding on a donkey's colt.

People

All hail the Messiah, King Jesus!

Leader

He has come to usher in a new, upside-down kingdom,
where the first is made last and the last made first.

People

All hail the Messiah, King Jesus!

Leader

He came not to overthrow governments or politicians,
but to rebelliously overturn
the powers of evil, fear, and death.

All

All hail the Messiah, King Jesus!

Prayer

*(Praising Jesus as True King/asking that his kingdom
come.)*

Song #1

" _____ " by _____.

upbeat, focused on the theme, familiar

Song #2

" _____ " by _____.

more contemplative, medium energy

Corporate Prayer of Confession

Leader

Gracious God, we come before you now
to confess that we have sinned against you
in our thoughts, words, and deeds—
by what we have done and what we have left undone.

Jesus, we confess to our desire
for an un-Christlike Messiah.
Like the Hebrews, we want something other than a
peaceful king on a donkey's colt.

All

Forgive us for not recognizing you as the True King.

Leader

In our sinful pride, we craft a savior of our own making,

a king in our own image,
and we pledge our allegiance to a false god
who fits into a narrative that is nothing like the
kingdom you spoke of and ushered in.

All
Forgive us for not recognizing you as the True King.

Leader
In our blindness, we fail to see your lordship,
and our mistake leaves a world of heartache, war, and
pain in its wake.

All
Forgive us for not recognizing you as the True King.

Leader
But thanks be to God
that you are truly the Messiah and King,
and that you are not always what we want you to be,
but something so much better:
a savior who came not in power and glory,
but in humility and grace,
so that we might know you as the caring,
gracious God that you are,
and that we might be forgiven and redeemed. Amen.

Song #3

" _____ " by _____ .

reflective, introspective, lower energy

Reading From Scripture

Song #4

" _____ " by _____ .

connects with the passage of Scripture, medium energy

Response to the Word

Song #5

" _____ " by _____ .

focus on God as Redeemer and Deliverer, medium-building energy

Benediction
May the peace of our Lord Jesus Christ
go with you as a blessing,
comfort, conviction, and a charge:
to always fight for justice,
pray for healing,
and listen for God.

LITURGIES

IN THE NAME OF THE SPIRIT

"To you, O people, I call out;
I raise my voice to all mankind.
You who are simple, gain prudence;
you who are foolish, set your hearts on it.
Listen, for I have trustworthy things to say;
I open my lips to speak what is right.
My mouth speaks what is true,
for my lips detest wickedness.
All the words of my mouth are just;
none of them is crooked or perverse.
To the discerning all of them are right;
they are upright to those who have found knowledge.
Choose my instruction instead of silver,
knowledge rather than choice gold,
for wisdom is more precious than rubies,
and nothing you desire can compare with her."

Proverbs 8:4-11 (NIV)

A Liturgy on the Spirit

Objectives:

1. To acknowledge and invite the Holy Spirit into our worship.
2. To encounter the Spirit of the Living God in a new and fresh way.
3. To be filled with and guided by the Holy Spirit.

Scripture:

1. Joel 2:28-32
2. Acts 2:1-12
3. Romans 8:1-17

Call to Worship

Leader

Spirit of God, we thank you for calling us to worship
today—for putting on our hearts the desire to gather,
to sing, to pray, and to love each other.

People

We respond to God's call with praise!

Leader

We know that this desire is not in our own nature,
it's not our natural inclination to gather as we do,
but your Spirit calls us to come and be made new.

People

We respond to God's call with praise!

Leader

When we accept this call, we know that you
are faithful to your promise,
and that by faith, obedience, and love
we are being formed into the image of Christ.

All

So let us join in faith and love
and respond to God's call with praise!

Song #1

" _____ " by _____ .

upbeat, familiar

Prayer of Invocation

(Asking the Spirit of God to come guide and form us.)

Song #2

" _____ " by _____ .

focus on the Holy Spirit

Song #3

" _____ " by _____ .

more contemplative, medium energy

Lectio Divina

Response to the Word

Song #4

" _____ " by _____ .

reflective, introspective, lower energy

Song #5

"_____" by _____.
well-known song, medium- to high-energy

Benediction
May the peace of our Lord Jesus Christ
go with you as a blessing,
comfort, conviction, and a charge:
to always fight for justice,
pray for healing,
and listen for God.

A Liturgy on Rest

Objectives:

1. To cease from our constant toil and striving.
2. To release the stress and pressure of our day-to-day lives to God.
3. To let Jesus replace our heavy burden with his light yoke.

Scripture:

1. Psalm 23:1-6
2. Matthew 11:28-30
3. Hebrews 4:1-11

Call to Worship

Today we want to acknowledge God's invitation for us
to rest our weary souls in him and relinquish the weight
of all that we've been carrying this week from our world,
our nation, our work, and our families.
As we think about and practice resting in God together,
we're going to begin our time with something called a
breath prayer:
an ancient Christian practice in which we use our breath
to focus our minds on resting and connecting with God.
The Holy Spirit is often described as the "breath" of
God, and as we breathe intentionally together, we are
acknowledging God's Spirit flowing in and through us.

Please, listen as I read Matthew 11:28-30 three times
through, and respond each time simply by breathing
in—imagining the life and peace of God flowing
in—and breathing out—imagining stress and anxiety
flowing out.

*"Come to me, all you who are weary and burdened, and I will
give you rest. Take my yoke upon you and learn from me, for I
am gentle and humble in heart, and you will find rest for your
souls. For my yoke is easy and my burden is light."* (NIV)

"Breathing in the life and peace of God" (inhale).

"Breathing out stress and anxiety" (exhale).

Repeat this two more times.

Prayer

(Ask God to give us rest.)

Song #1

"_____" by _____.

upbeat, focused on the theme, familiar

Song #2

"_____" by _____.

more contemplative, medium energy

Corporate Prayer of Confession

Leader

Gracious God, we come before you now
to confess that we have sinned against you
in our thoughts,
words, and deeds—
by what we have done
and what we have left undone.

We confess to living lives of hectic frenzy, O Lord.
Consumed by productivity, we seek validation
in what we do rather than who we are in you.

All

Forgive us for not resting in the work of Jesus.

Leader

We strive and stretch our thin-to-breaking souls,
filling our lives with task upon life-draining task
and one-upping each other with the fullness of our days,
always boasting in our capacity to carry more.

All

Forgive us for not resting in the work of Jesus.

Leader

It is good to work hard and labor,
but this failure to be idle has become our idol,
and our trust in you, O Lord,
is weaker than the trust we place
in our own ability to care for ourselves.

All

Forgive us for not resting in the work of Jesus.

Leader

But thanks be to God that the work of Jesus *is* enough.
Because of his life, death, and resurrection,
we don't have to work "hard enough" to justify ourselves
to God or anyone else.
In the work of Jesus, we can truly rest. Amen.

Song #3

" _____ " by _____.

reflective, introspective, lower energy

Reading From Scripture

Song #4

" _____ " by _____.

connects with the passage of Scripture, medium energy

Response to the Word

Song #5

" _____ " by _____.

focus on God as Redeemer and Deliverer, medium- to low-building energy

Benediction
May the peace of our Lord Jesus Christ
go with you as a blessing,
comfort, conviction, and a charge:
to always fight for justice,
pray for healing,
and listen for God.

A Liturgy on Lament

Objectives:

1. To introduce the concept of lament and its importance.
2. To facilitate a space where these emotions and cries to God may be expressed.
3. To ground our concept and expression of lament in the hope of God's goodness.

Scripture:

1. Lamentations 3:13-24
2. Psalm 13
3. John 11:17-37

Into Lament

Today's theme and direction for our time worshipping together centers around lament:
an internal and external cry directed toward God in response to the pain, brokenness, and evil we see and experience in our world.
Lament is not "woe is me" self-pity, but an honest and vulnerable expression of our need and reliance on God to rescue, redeem, and restore us.
We ask these things in faith and celebrate God's goodness and faithfulness, but in this time together, we also acknowledge that sometimes there is no happy ending on earth,
and that in those moments God is still good, loving, and faithful.

Psalm 69 (NLT) gives us a great example of what it looks like to cry out to God in lament while still trusting and hoping in his love and salvation. The psalmist says:

"But I keep praying to you, Lord,
hoping this time you will show me favor.
In your unfailing love, O God,
answer my prayer with your sure salvation.
Rescue me from the mud;
don't let me sink any deeper!
Save me from those who hate me,
and pull me from these deep waters.
Don't let the floods overwhelm me,

or the deep waters swallow me,
or the pit of death devour me.

"Answer my prayers, O Lord,
for your unfailing love is wonderful.
Take care of me,
for your mercy is so plentiful.
Don't hide from your servant;
answer me quickly, for I am in deep trouble!
Come and redeem me;
free me from my enemies."

(vv. 13-18)

Prayer

(Asking that God would help us all enter into this space of lament.)

Song #1

"_____" by _____.
low- to medium energy, focuses on the theme, familiar

Corporate Prayer of Lament

Leader
What, O Lord, can fulfill this hunger?

What can renew the dryness in our souls?
We long to be filled, and spend our lives searching
for something, anything to fill the void.

People

But all that we strive after fades in the sun.
All that we chase is dissolved as a mist.

Leader

What, O Lord, can quench this thirst?
What can satisfy the desires of our hearts?
We long to be submerged in the stream of life,
and to drink deeply from the fountain of blessing.

People

But all of our toil is done in vain.
All of our labor is found to be meaningless.

Leader

Where, O Lord, are righteousness and justice found?
Where can we look to find healing and wholeness?
We long to see your kingdom come here on earth as it is
in heaven.

People

But our sense of justice is perverted,
and all that we do accomplishes little.

Leader

All our work is meaningless apart from you, O Lord.
Fulfill our hunger and quench our thirst

that we might find meaning and healing in the fullness
of the life that you offer
as we work alongside you. Amen.

Song #2

"_____" by _____.

reflective, introspective, lower energy

Reading from Scripture

Song #3

"_____" by _____.

connects with the passage of Scripture, medium- to low-energy

Response to the Word

Song #4

"_____" by _____.

focus on God as Redeemer and Deliverer, medium-building energy

Benediction

May the peace of our Lord Jesus Christ
go with you as a blessing,
comfort, conviction, and a charge:
to always fight for justice,
pray for healing,
and listen for God.

A Liturgy on Silence

Objectives:

1. To quiet our busy minds and hearts in the presence of God.
2. To listen for the still, small voice of God.
3. To practice a deep and contemplative focus on the goodness and love of God.

Scripture:

1. 1 Kings 19:9b-18
2. Matthew 6:1-7
3. Romans 8:18-30

Call to Worship

Leader (from 1 Kings 9:11-13)
*"Go out and stand before me on the mountain," the L*ORD
*told Elijah, and as he stood there, the L*ORD *passed by, and a
mighty windstorm hit the mountain. It was such a terrible
blast that the rocks were torn loose…*

People
*But the L*ORD *was not in the wind…*

Leader
After the wind there was an earthquake…

People
*But the L*ORD *was not in the earthquake…*

Leader
And after the earthquake there was a fire…

People
*But the L*ORD *was not in the fire…*

Leader
*And after the fire there was the sound of a gentle whisper.
When Elijah heard it, he wrapped his face in his cloak and
went out and stood
at the entrance of the cave.
And a voice said,
"What are you doing here, Elijah?"*

Prayer & Silence

Leader

Prayer: "Teach us to listen for you in the silence, O Lord. Tune our ears to the gentle whisper of your voice."

Please take a moment now in silent prayer,
simply listening for the still,
small voice of the one who asks, "What are you doing here?"

Song #1

" _____ " by _____.

more contemplative, medium energy

Silence

("Now I want to invite you to take a moment in silence before God.")

Prayer of Silent Confession

Leader

Prayer: Gracious God, we come before you now to confess that we have sinned against you in our thoughts, words, and deeds—by what we have done and what we have left undone.

We confess that in this world of chaos, noise, and clamor, Lord, we have forgotten how to sit with you in silence. We no longer listen for your still, small voice in the quiet of the early morning or the soft hush of later evening. We go about our days in a cacophony of raucous events and errands, the manic noise in our lives reflected in the churning waters of our minds. Forgive us for neglecting to be still with you.

Now, please take a few moments of silent reflection and confession before God.

Song #3

" _____ " by _____.
reflective, introspective, lower energy

Reading from Scripture

Silence
("Please take a moment to silently reflect on the Word of God.")

Response to the Word

Song #5

" _____ " by _____.

focus on God as Redeemer and Deliverer, medium- to low-building energy

Benediction

May the peace of our Lord Jesus Christ
go with you as a blessing,
comfort, conviction, and a charge:
to always fight for justice,
pray for healing,
and listen for God.